HOW MUSCLES LEARN:
TEACHING THE VIOLIN
WITH THE BODY IN MIND

HOW MUSCLES LEARN:
TEACHING THE VIOLIN WITH THE BODY IN MIND

By

Susan Kempter

Alfred Music
P.O. Box 10003
Van Nuys, CA 91410-0003
alfred.com

ISBN-10: 1-58951-401-7
ISBN-13: 978-1-58951-401-0

Cover Design and Photographs by Jane Soyka

"I'm happy to recommend Susan Kempter's book, HOW MUSCLES LEARN, as a welcome addition to violin pedagogy. Ms. Kempter addresses problems of relaxation and body posture in the early stages of development – an area which is woefully neglected by many teachers of beginners. The key to violinistic longevity is the ability to play with maximum ease and relaxation. This book deals with that ultimate goal.

— Leonard Felberg, Professor of Violin Emeritus,
University of New Mexico

"Combining her substantial training and personal research in the subjects of anatomy and physiology with a successful string teaching philosophy, Susan Kempter offers a unique perspective to conscientious string teachers. Through illustrations, photos and language, many common problems of violin playing that deal with the body and its use are identified, their detrimental effects are explored, and solutions offered. No matter what approach or favorite techniques a teacher embraces, this book will provide food for thought, and undoubtedly open new avenues to consider. No string teacher's vision is complete without it!"

— Lorraine Fink, author, violinist and Suzuki
Teacher Trainer

"...a treasure of information about the physical factors in violin study, written with a superb knowledge of physiology and kinesiology, and yet easily understandable to the reader without a background in exercise science. It should be part of every string pedagogy course."

— Kari Gunderson, Myofacial Therapist and
Professor of String Pedagogy, Ohio State
University

"What an exciting new look at the development of technique – definitely unique among the available resources for teachers...The balance between principles and applications to violin playing and learning is just right. I am already viewing several of my current teaching challenges with new perspectives."

— Margaret Hawn, violinist and Suzuki specialist

f

Foreward

Muscles and bodies can be, and ought to be, thoroughly trained, and they should be trained before concentrating exclusively on musical outcomes. Teaching movements to be fluid, postures to be stress-free and balanced and teaching students and parents what to look for to achieve these ends can be a constructive and fulfilling musical experience for young children and a necessary part of the mechanics of playing for older beginners and adults.

Acknowledgments

This book was made possible by a Research and Creative Work grant from the College of Fine Arts at the University of New Mexico.

Photography, layout and cover design: Jane Soyka

I would like to thank the following for their advice and insight in reviewing the manuscript:

    Lorraine Fink, violinist and Suzuki pedagogue

    Helen Higa, violinist and Alexander specialist

    John Kendall, pedagogue, friend and mentor

    Nancy Uscher, Professor of Music & Associate Provost for Academic Affairs, University of New Mexico

    Lynn Medoff, M.A., M.P.T., for reviewing the manuscript and her generosity in allowing the use of a portion of her article.

Don Robertson for the use of his recital hall for the photographs.

Models for photographs: Tom Beer, Rachel Fleischer, Natalie Fleischer, Heath French, Morgan French, Sarah Rhodes, Amy Romero and Justin Robertson.

Preface

While this book was written as a text for part of my String Pedagogy Program at the University of New Mexico, I have been surprised and delighted at the interest shown by my colleagues.

No book can do justice to all the research related to motor programs and how muscles learn. My intention is that information of this sort will be useful in helping teachers find productive techniques that enhance approaches they are comfortable with, and possibly offer a few insights into some of their frustrations.

Contents

To Dale, Melissa, Jeff and Sarah, and to my students
who continue to teach me.

Introduction

During my graduate studies at the University of New Mexico, I was fortunate to be able to pursue several diverse subjects not usually associated with string teaching. One of these subjects was an in-depth inquiry into how muscles learn movement patterns and how our awareness can modify those patterns. Combined with previous course work in human anatomy and physiology, extensive personal reading and many sessions with Alexander specialists, I began to notice that even though the language and/or approaches differed, there seemed to be a few principles about which these disciplines appeared to agree. These principles are the core of this publication, which is not meant to be a course in kinesthetics, Alexander, biomechanics or physiology, but rather an approach to teaching the violin.

For the sake of clarification, a brief description/definition of the following might be helpful:

The Alexander Method/Technique: An "owner's or operation manual" which helps students to re-educate and restore beneficial postures and movements. It engages the mind and body to reduce and eliminate body misuse in daily activities.

Physiology: A branch of biology that deals with organic/bodily processes in living organisms. Most of these processes are unconscious. Examples might be biochemical transmission of nutrients and electrolytes, composition/function of fluids in the body.

Kinesiology: The study of muscles during movement. For our purposes, we will define these as conscious movements, or those under willful control. Examples might be opening a door or pouring cream into your coffee.

Biomechanics: A link between biology and physics that investigates movements from the perspective of joint and muscular design. Examples might be range of motion studies of various joints and optimal angles/pressures to accomplish certain tasks.

Physical Therapy: The treatment of disease or injury by physical and/or mechanical means. Examples might be movement therapy, massage, heat treatments.

Researchers in each of these fields, as well as many others, are interested in the workings of the human body, and all have a potential contribution to make to upper string teachers and players. For violinists and violists, the effort to obtain "hands on" information from all the potential sources can be difficult and time-consuming, especially since the research must be ferreted out, read, interpreted and then finally applied to violin playing. An added frustration is that most musicians are not trained in research methodologies and do not understand the language in which most research is written. An additional complication is that violin and viola teaching tends to focus on performance, whether in public school programs, universities, conservatories, private studios, summer camps, institutes, or master classes. Oftentimes, the means whereby any performance is achieved are overlooked, or taken for granted until injury or discomfort occur. All of these reasons, combined with the time necessary for daily practice, make a reasonable argument why more upper string players have not sought out this data.

Researchers Frank Wilson and Franz Roehmann acknowledge that because of the multidisciplinary nature of the problem, it is difficult to ferret out meaningful or pertinent information…"there is no such thing as a 'field' of movement science; instead, there is an ad hoc and shifting affiliation of psychologists, biomechanical engineers, mathematicians, anthropologists, prosthesis and robot builders, cockpit designers, sports and dance trainers, neurologists and neurophysiologists, physical therapists, Feldenkrais and Alexander practitioners, and sundry stationary human workstation ergonomists. Consequently, were music educators interested in a serious working relationship with movement scientists, the realization (and the achievements) of such a collaboration would depend almost entirely on chance." [Wilson & Roehmann, 1992, p 510]

Perhaps because the necessary information is difficult to obtain, and perhaps because musical study has focused on performance outcomes instead of the body producing them, there is a dearth of information about training the bodies of upper string students. This seems to be an appalling omission, given the intensity and duration with which many violinists drive their bodies.

For me, the inquiry began many years ago when I began carrying binoculars to every concert and recital I attended. Although it wasn't particularly kosher, I carefully observed concert artists, and took in every detail of their performance. It became as wonderful for me to observe well-trained bodies as it was to hear beautiful music. I never saw a great virtuoso who did not exhibit fluid, balanced movements associated with performance, although the rare example surely exists. I used to wonder if all great violinists were naturally coordinated, and if that was the determining factor that allowed supreme virtuosity to emerge. Certainly, those of us who have taught for many years know that some students come to the instrument with more grace and ease and less tension than others. Yet, those same years of teaching have also shown me that many of my finest students have struggled with one or more physical aspects of their playing. These convictions have led me to a satisfying and fruitful teaching approach, especially for students who desired to play well and may not have initially demonstrated the innate ability to move in a coordinated non-injurious manner.

More recently, I had the privilege to watch Pinchas Zuckerman teaching students via digital broadcast between

Albuquerque and New York. The occasion was a ceremony introducing live digital broadcasts between the cities. What an extraordinary opportunity to be very close to him while he demonstrated for his students. Because of the nature of the broadcast, and the dignitaries present, I was compelled to sit quietly and observe. Again, I was struck with the ease with which he played. Each passage was executed with easy, fluid movements, and his body was in perfect balance in spite of the physical and musical demands of the pieces he was demonstrating.

The combination of my interest in the "science" of playing, the observations I had made and my dedication to teacher training prompted the writing of this book, the premise of which is that muscles and bodies can be, and ought to be, thoroughly trained, and that they should be trained before concentrating exclusively on musical outcomes.

Perhaps the most compelling rationale for this approach is to reduce the load on our students' working memory. Simply put, all conscious learning takes place within the very limited capacity of one's working memory system. The original research was done by G.A. Miller [Miller, 1956] in which he hypothesized that working memory is limited. It can only manage 5 to 9 bits of information at a time. Subsequent research has also indicated that EACH of the 5 to 9 bits must be rehearsed or practiced sufficiently to embed it into long term memory banks, where it can be easily recognized and recalled under favorable conditions.

From a practical point of view, this means that a student probably will not retain much if the lesson includes placement of right and left hands and feet, centering and elongating the spine, turning the head to situate it comfortably on the chin rest, attending to each finger of the bow hold, the octave frame of the left hand, and playing with a straight bow stroke, hitting only one string at a time, keeping the bow hair flat, counting each note correctly and playing in tune!

Although this list is not complete, it may help us appreciate how great the physical and cognitive demands on students might be.

Teaching the body to recognize and feel correct postures and positions stresses working memory – especially in the beginning. Only when the body becomes comfortable and balanced, and movements become practically unconscious can music playing begin to be the primary focus of the lessons.

Actually, teaching the body before teaching the music can be satisfying for both teacher and student because: 1. the need for rehabilitation is reduced; 2. students can measure progress in concrete, observable steps; 3. advanced music is more satisfying when it is played without tension; and 4. the ultimate pay-back is when advanced students have developed the controlled balance and fluid motions to play a great concerto or sonata with a technique that allows them to realize their own musical goals.

From a pedagogical point of view, this approach is especially productive with pre-school and elementary age children because they are "physical" learners. For most elementary age children, the thrill is in the "doing." They are focused on controlling their bodies in their immediate environment. They repeatedly try to tie shoe laces, stack blocks or ride a bike. Elementary children love skill mastery. They do not seek reasons, justifications or explanations the way older students or adults do. Teaching these youngsters presents a special opportunity for teachers. Why not honor where they are and teach via "what it feels/looks like, or what the muscle/hand/arm is doing?" Teaching movements to be fluid, postures to be stress-free and balanced and teaching students and parents what to look for to achieve these ends can be a constructive and fulfilling musical experience for young children and a necessary part of the mechanics of playing for older beginners and adults.

Since young children are "physical learners" this is a natural time to simplify the teaching approach. By concentrating on teaching the body first, a foundation and internal structure can be constructed onto which rhythm, tone production, phrasing, shifting, vibrato and advanced bow strokes can be successfully attached. "Sounds OK," you say, "but what about intonation? Why is that musical element missing?" The answer is that this teaching approach requires that the left hand be formed correctly and the fingers placed without tension in exactly the correct spot from the beginning. Intonation, therefore, becomes the first musical element to emerge from a well-balanced body, and is a constant from the beginning. Rhythm is a close second.

Suzuki teachers may argue this point because Suzuki students typically begin playing rhythms BEFORE they use any fingers. This is true. The reality, however, is that the manner in which the early rhythms are played and accomplished gradually changes over time. ♫♫♫ ♫ played by a young child might take two inches of bow in the square of the arm and actually be played like ♫♫♫ ♪♪ . As the child develops control, the length of the stroke increases and the integrity of the rhythm, as it is written, is gradually approximated until the student has a repertoire of possibilities when playing ♫♫♫ ♫ , the choice of which depends on the context in which the rhythmic fragment is found. On the other hand, a note is perceived (by the teacher, at first, and later by the student) to be "in tune," or "out of tune" individually, or in context. There is no such thing as gradually approximating intonation. Another way of putting it is that the bow stroke will change and refine itself over the course of years, but intonation is "stable." It either "is" or it "is not."

The figure on the next page shows how I view the process. With this image in mind, the coordinated body is fundamental for all musical skill and technique to develop. Notice how many skills are below "ground level" in the picture. Even though none of these foundational skills requires the student to play, each is an integral component of future technical development. For this reason, I do not

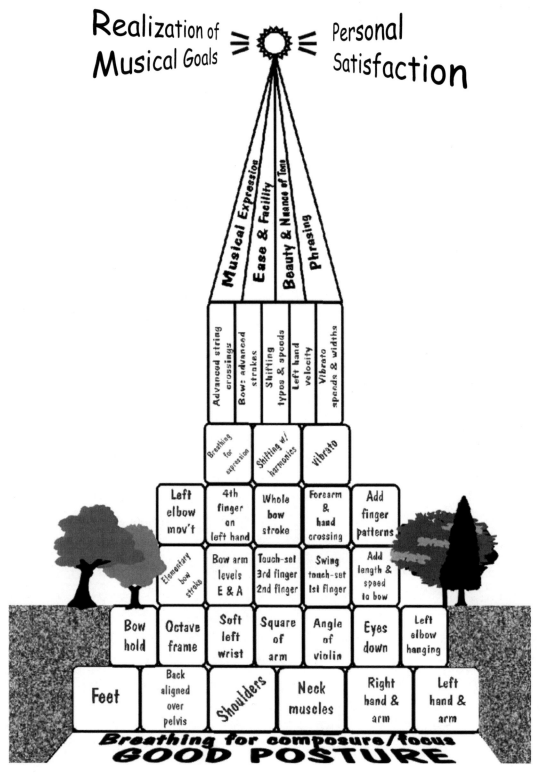

"Building" a Student

let any student play unless the body is ready, including what I call the "Basic 6":

- 1. Placement of the feet with heels directly under the thigh sockets

- 2. The trunk of the body is upright and pelvis is centered over the legs, shoulders are down in their normal, relaxed position, the back is elongated and the belly button is centered between the pelvic bones

- 3. The neck is free of tension

- 4. The right hand is holding the bow in "the best" bow hold the student can make

- 5. The left hand is at the correct height and is soft, with curved, separate fingers which fold easily over the fingerboard (called the "octave frame" of the left hand), and

- 6. The student is quiet and ready to receive instruction

> The physical set-up of the student consumes early lessons. If any of the above 6 physical aspects are not in place, they automatically take priority. For the first year or two, most of each lesson is devoted to these issues. As the body learns, postures and positions become more automatic, and more and more lesson time can be devoted to traditional music teaching, including phrasing, interpretation and music literacy.

Since articulate control of muscles and ease of movement are integral parts of playing well, a strong link between brain and body must be established, which I believe begins with good posture. I am reminded of Lauren Sosniak's article from the *Proceedings of the 1987 Denver Conference on Music and Child Development.* In her study, twenty one concert artists (pianists) were interviewed about factors contributing to their professional success. One of the discoveries she made was the amount of time it took for them to achieve international recognition. "(They) worked for an average of 17 years from their first formal lessons to their international recognition. The fastest 'made it' in 12 years; the slowest took 25." [Sosniak, 1990, p. 277]

If we assume that most of the students with whom we work have at least the potential of the concert artists in Sosniak's study, we might be less hurried to teach the "music," and more committed to teach the body. Fluid motions, light touch and natural balance take time to teach. My own experience has been that it takes four to seven years. This may seem like a long time to really concentrate on "teaching the body," but the ratio of time spent teaching the physical aspects are not out of proportion to the total time spent studying, and the students are still playing music. If the average concert artist interviewed by Lauren Sosniak took 17 years to reach the concert stage, then 4 years in training the body would represent approximately 23% of the invested time. Seven years would be approximately 42% of the 17 years.

These percentages certainly seem reasonable considering that the quality of sound produced depends largely upon the body's ability to produce it, which is at least as important as the desire to play well. Of course, we must not discount the numbers of upper string players who have experienced pain and/or injury. Teaching students to be aware of movement patterns as well as postures and angles that are "user friendly" might also help reduce the number of players who get injured or have discomfort when playing. Even when it takes longer than four years, it is time well-spent. We can, after all, have students who play with grace and ease, or students who play awkwardly and/or with maladaptive movement patterns. The outcome is often in the hands of teachers.

This is not to say that every student will consistently play optimally; some students, no matter how much they have been shown, nagged or video taped, continue to play with less than desirable movements. These students, while progressing, never go beyond "OK." I have never been able to introduce them to the virtuoso literature. Instead, we continually struggle with shifting, vibrato, string crossings and the mechanics of playing in the student repertoire. Of course, this is frustrating for me and for the student, who sees his peers progressing into advanced repertoire.

Teaching the body can be a challenge to teachers who feel that adhering to notation and/or accurate musical reproduction is the IMMEDIATE goal of instruction. Certainly, accuracy in intonation and rhythm are desired by any string teacher. The difference being considered here is in how willing one might be to delay the musical instruction in favor of the physical instruction which must precede it.

Another point to consider is that from a cognitive point of view, it is more realistic to have students focusing on one or two aspects of their playing than on several. The latter runs the risk of overloading limited Working Memory resources.

 In defense of teachers, however, it is difficult to teach what has never been learned. As long as teacher preparation courses continue to neglect physiology, kinesthetics and movement analysis as part of their curriculum, little will change in the studio or classroom.

Since pedagogy is a necessary requirement for students majoring in Music Education and in Performance, it seems reasonable that an overview of human anatomy, physiology, kinesthetics and their applications to violin playing and teaching be offered. Perhaps this neglect helps explain Wilson and Roehmann's statement, "The teacher's job, of course, is not to defend or explain pedagogical practice but to produce musicians…" [Wilson & Roehmann, 1992, p 511] Their observation might serve as a wake up call for all violin teachers to become familiar with the bodies with which they work as well as with the music they teach.

It is hoped that the following principles, and their applications, will help teachers know what to look for, and what to avoid. It is also hoped that teachers will experiment with these principles, develop more approaches and teaching strategies … and then share them!

Things to think about...

1. On page 7 is a figure entitled "Building a Student." This figure contains 14 blocks that represent skills upon which future techniques are built. List five activities for each that would help students develop those skills.

2. Devise a 10 minute teaching segment on intonation for a "physical learner." Do not use note names, intervals, key signatures, etc.

3. If you have access to an elementary-age student, videotape yourself teaching a lesson to a physical learner. Use simple, concrete language that helps the child understand what his/her body needs to do. Avoid using any words or musical terminology the child doesn't understand.

Principle Number One...

The Importance of Good Posture

Consideration of the Nose, Elbow, Scroll and Toe:

Most violin teachers repeatedly tell their students to "stand up straight," knowing intuitively that good posture is the basis for good playing. Some teachers have tried to simplify the teaching of posture by insisting that each of their students, regardless of body type, stand with Nose, left Elbow, violin Scroll and the left Toe vertically aligned (NEST). While such a posture might work for some body builds, it is by no means a cure-all for everyone, and is not a quick fix for the posture dilemma.

Well-balanced posture is more than standing up straight, or aligning nose, elbow, scroll and toe vertically — either of which has the potential of producing tensions and/or less-than-optimal movement patterns. Good posture must be analyzed on an individual basis. The best description of points to look for in establishing good posture in violinists was recently published in the journal, Medical Problems of Performing Artists [December, 1999] by Lynn Medoff, M.A., M.P.T.

Extreme tension in neck (sternoclydomastoidal muscle, usually called SCM) —

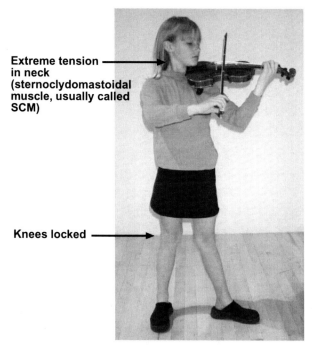

Sway-back or lordosis of spine ←

Knees locked →

Although the above student looks impressive, tension in the back and neck are readily apparent.

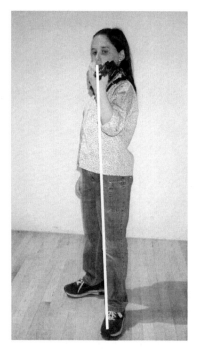

This student has a body build that allows the NEST to work: Knees are not locked, the neck is not stressed, and the back is centered over the pelvic bones.

The following excerpt is re-printed here with Lynn Medoff's permission:

PROPER POSTURE

...The trunk, the head, and the extremities (the arms and the legs) make up the skeletal framework. The trunk consists of three units of weight: the shoulder girdle, rib cage, and pelvis. Along with the head, these units are organized around and supported by a central axis, the spinal column. The main part of the spinal column is made up of 24 vertebral bodies (7 cervical, 12 thoracic, 5 lumbar), which stack up to form a long, flexible column of continuous and opposing curves. When the body is well balanced, the spine closely approximates the center axis of the body through which weight falls. The weight of the head, shoulder girdle, and rib cage is transferred to the spinal column and carried downward to the pelvis and then to the legs. Weight transfer through the body is cumulative. It is therefore essential to properly position the pelvis, which is at the base of the spinal column. When the trunk is well balanced, weight flows easily downward through the long balanced curves of the spinal column. Minimal effort, in the form of muscular work, is needed to maintain balance (Fig. A).

FIG. A. Organization of posture around central axis. When the body is balanced and centered, it is organized close to and around a central axis, which efficiently carries the weight downward.

Babies instinctively understand how to balance as they move through the stages of sitting, crawling, standing and walking. Humans generally lose this ability as they age and fall into slumped, inefficient postures. This may be due to the enormous task of maintaining the upright posture, misconceptions about proper posture, and/or the adaptation of a sedentary lifestyle. Most people vacillate between two postures, the "strain and the slouch," in an attempt to win the fight against gravity. The former posture has too much tension, the latter not enough. Both postures are inefficient.

The following "balanced posture" images based on Sweigard's "lines-of-movement" are designed to aid visualization of good body posture.

Balanced Alignment

Balanced Sitting Posture

- The pelvis is vertical and balanced on the center of the two rounded bones at its bottom. It is neither tilted forward, causing the lower back to sway, nor tilted back, causing the buttocks to tuck under.

- The lumbar curve assumes a forward curve.

- The rib cage hangs down toward the pelvis.

- The shoulder girdle rests on top of the rib cage and the shoulders are relaxed.

- The chest floats up and the upper body widens.

- To position the head properly, the spinal column lengthens upward through the center of the neck as the head floats up to balance on top of it.

Balanced Standing Posture

- The feet are placed directly under the thigh sockets (about 6 inches apart) with the toes facing approximately straight ahead.

- The knees are relaxed and in line with the thigh and ankle joints.

- The pelvis rests on top of the thighs and is neither pushed forward nor tilted back.

- The trunk is balanced as in the sitting posture.

- The arms hang long at the sides.

Balance, once achieved, must be maintained. This is accomplished via "centering." "Centering" is the ability to maintain equilibrium by balancing the external compressive and internal tensile forces acting upon the body. Irmgard Bartenieff was a dancer and physical therapist who applied Laban's philosophies to her work. She describes "centering" as "being able to connect with the source of one's strength (support) even when in motion so that balance is maintained in all activities." For Bartenieff, as Laban, centering is crucial for the maintenance of dynamic alignment.

The body's anatomical center of gravity is located within the pelvis. Sweigard likens the pelvis to the hub of a wheel. The upper and lower extremities are the spokes of the wheel. The legs are attached directly to the pelvis at the thigh sockets and the arms are attached indirectly to the pelvis through muscle and fascial connective sheaths. Like the hub, the pelvis is the center of control for movement. When stabilized properly, the pelvis initiates and controls movement. Bartenieff states that movement takes on form when it is initiated from the center and its shape is maintained if the central point of reference remains strong. Alignment, which is centered and balanced, allows movement to be realized without overexertion and stress.

POSTURAL FAULTS IN VIOLINISTS:

Many biomedical faults of the upper body are due to improper alignment of the lower body, particularly the pelvis. However, violin teachers often ignore the lower body while focusing correction on upper-body position. The shoulder girdle is the supportive framework for the upper extremities. It must be balanced to ensure fluid, efficient arm movement. Its balance is dependent upon good

a   b

Fig. B. Postural faults in violinists. Note the subtle differences between postures **a** and **b**. Postural faults present in **a**: knees are hyperextended, hips are swayed forward, lower back is hollowed out, shoulders are behind pelvis, left elbow is too close to the body, and chin is forcibly tucked in to compensate for forward head posture; **b**: corrected posture.

trunk alignment, which occurs only when the pelvis is positioned properly. Pelvic position, in turn, is influenced by the placement of the legs. Thus, lower-body alignment should always be addressed when correcting upper-body posture and mechanics, e.g., a left elbow that is shoved too far forward may be due to a posteriorly tilted pelvis (hips swayed forward). The following corrections are often necessary to change postural faults common to adolescent and young adult violinists (Fig. B).

Correction of Standing Posture

- *Foot placement: The left foot is turned out slightly so that the toes point in the direction of the scroll instead of pointing straight ahead. Body weight is over the toes instead of the heels to facilitate weight transfer.*

- *Knee position: The knees are relaxed and flexible instead of locked and rigid.*

- *Pelvic position: The pelvis (the body's center) hangs under the rib cage and balances on top of the legs. It is stabilized by a lengthened contraction of the abdominal muscles to prevent the most common positional fault of swaying the hips forward.*

- *Low back: The lumbar spine assumes a slight forward curve when the pelvis is position properly. When the pelvis tips forward into an anterior tilt, the lumbar curve becomes exaggerated; when it tips back into a posterior tilt, the curve becomes flattened.*

- *Chest, upper back, and rib cage: The chest and upper back are open and broad instead of sunken and rounded forward, causing the rib cage, sternum, and clavicle to sink. This should not be achieved by pinching the scapulae together.*

- *Shoulders: There is width between the shoulders, which are relaxed to allow weight to drop into the elbows. They should not be elevated or pulled forward.*

- *Scapulae: The scapulae relax downward on the back; their inner borders are neither pulled inward toward the spine nor allowed to migrate too far forward on the rib cage, as often happens with rounded shoulders and a sunken chest.*

- *Head and neck: The neck is lengthened and the head floats upward to balance on top of the spine, instead of hanging forward.*

- *The arms: When the pelvis, rib cage and shoulder girdle are relaxed and balanced, weight falls easily from the shoulder girdle to the arms. The elbows are weighted and move freely. The left elbow should not lock into a forward position and the right elbow should not be held too high.*

Sizing the Violin:

Another factor affecting correct posture is the size of the instrument, which is a matter of concern for all violin teachers. Perhaps it is of most importance when working with young children because they do not have the stamina of adults. Instruments that are too long, too wide or too heavy, especially for young children, can cause a variety of tensions which might have undesirable results.

Teachers do not universally agree how the instrument should be sized. Some feel that if the middle finger of the hand can extend itself around the scroll and/or into the peg box, or if the hand can be reached around the peg box, the size of the instrument is OK.

Sizing instrument by placing middle finger in peg box.

Sizing instrument by reaching hand around scroll.

Looking at these same students in first position (below) shows the necessity of extending their left arms beyond a comfortable supportable angle.

Such an extension tends to increase tension in the neck, shoulders and arms. Students may compensate by complaining that they are tired when playing, or by drooping, which allows the upper arm to rest against the body. This drooping posture increases the strain on the muscles of the neck and shoulders.

In the photos below, the tendency to drop the upper arm against the body in order to support the weight and length of the large instrument is demonstrated. Notice how the left shoulder is pulled downward by the upper arm pressing against the body.

The uncomfortable extension of the left arm will encourage student to drop the upper arm against the body in order to support the weight and length of the instrument.

Although there is no rule that seems to hold for every student, the following two criteria seem to be helpful:

1. Determine the length of the violin:

Sizing the violin by keeping the scroll inside a watch band.

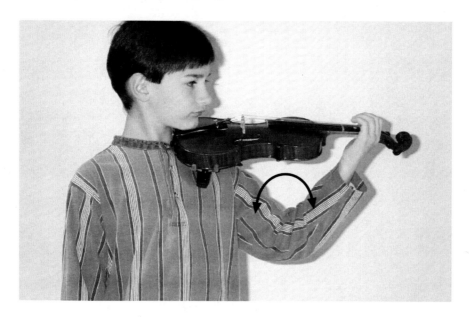

Sizing the violin by observing the angle of forearm and upper arm. It should be approximately 90° when student is in first position.

2. Determine the width of the violin:

Teachers should note the width of the lower bout in relation to the size of the body of the student.

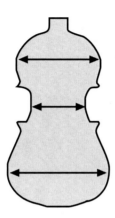

Diagram showing the three bouts of the violin.

If the instrument protrudes over the back of the left shoulder, or over the sternum (a wide, flat bone running down the midline of the front of the body over the chest, also sometimes called the breastbone), it might hamper easy, light movements of the left hand and arm because of its width. Of course, the bigger the instrument, the more the student has to support, and the more the tendency for tension or poor posture.

When placing an instrument on a student, imagine the sternum and then observe where the lower bout of the instrument is in relation to it.

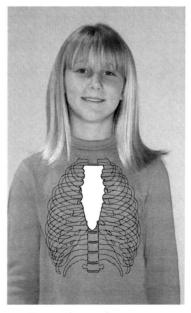

Location of sternum

Notice how the bout of this large violin impinges upon the sternum.

Other considerations that impact posture are the choices of shoulder pads and chinrests. It is the responsibility of the teacher to have sponges, scissors, pads and sandpaper readily available so that instruments can be comfortably "fit" to each student.

Most chinrests can be sanded to remove too large bumps or to reduce length slightly. Always finish with very fine sandpaper or 000-steel wool to return the chinrest to a satin finish.

Think of this process as akin to selecting a pair of walking shoes. We would not think of buying a pair of shoes that forced us to walk on the outside edges of our feet or with toes curled up. Instead, we shop until we find shoes that are comfortable and promote balance and good posture when we walk. Furthermore, we buy new shoes when the need arises. I think of the set-up of the violin just like this. Once a student has a properly-sized instrument, then the work of making him/her comfortable begins.

It has been my experience that most students are more comfortable using some sort of support under the violin. This is optional, however, AS LONG AS TENSION IN NECK AND SHOULDERS CAN BE COMPLETELY AVOIDED. Some students who might not initially need a shoulder pad might grow in such a way that one is needed later on – another reason for years of careful observation by teachers.

Chinrests and shoulder pads come in several shapes and sizes, but they do not come adapted to each body that needs them. I find that most students need some customizing of chinrests and shoulder pads. We should take very seriously the approach that Alexander teachers tell us…"bring the instrument to the body, not the body to the instrument." My translation of that is that each instrument must be made "user friendly" given the body playing it. If we think of setting and maintaining good posture, some potential stresses can be avoided. But the entire body of the student must also be addressed.

Angles of the Head:

As Lynn Medoff advised, the angle of the head is very important. This can be seen from the front or back, but can be seen especially well from the back of the student. An easy way to visualize a correct angle is to see whether the head tilts toward or away from the violin.

Teachers must constantly watch for the angle at which the head contacts the violin. This becomes problematic when students try to look at tapes placed on the fingerboards of their instruments, or try to read music when the music stand and the student's body are not properly aligned. Suzuki teachers must be keenly aware of this because students are often told to "watch the tapes," then told, "don't let your head fall over." It is a problem uniquely associated with our instrument, and quick fixes are not readily available. We must, therefore, be diligent in placing jaws in chinrests, and teaching students (and parents, if they are available) to watch for soft neck muscles and shoulders that are relaxed and back in their natural position. Another help is for teachers to tell students that their eyes will gradually accommodate to not being centered on the tapes… and to begin using their ears more and eyes less.

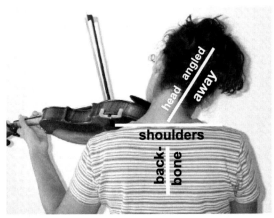

Incorrect angle, showing head tilted away from the violin.

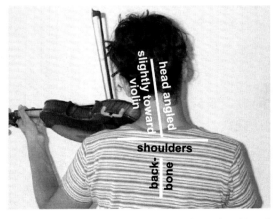

Correct angle, showing head tilted toward the violin.

 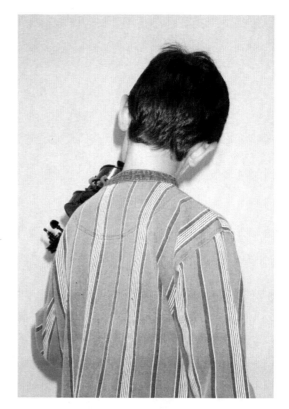

Notice in both of the photos above that the chin, rather than the jaw, seems to be in the chinrest. Also note the resulting odd angle of the head.

Maybe this is a good time to begin calling it a "jaw rest."

To understand what the student is experiencing, teachers may try the following exercise, as illustrated in the photo on page 26, Pretend to hold your violin ON YOUR RIGHT SHOULDER. Now, hold a book in the right hand approximately where tapes would be on a violin and attempt to read for several minutes. While reading, keep your head slightly slanted toward the imaginary violin and keep neck soft, shoulders down and back in their natural position.

 Teachers, you must do this with the violin on the "wrong" shoulder, because your eyes have probably accommodated to the usual side. The visual discomfort you feel is exactly what your students experience while trying to "watch the tapes." In order to center the visual field (and relieve the strain on the eyes), students often twist their necks in very unnatural positions. This is a good reason to get the left hand trained as quickly as possible, thus reducing their need to "watch."

Angles of the Violin:

Occasionally, odd angles are produced, not because of the visual discomfort of the student, but because of skinny little bodies and sloping shoulders. In these cases, no matter which shoulder pad is chosen, the violin will be at too great an angle for the bow arm to have easy access to the E string, or be able to apply weight to the E string. When we encounter a problem like this, it is helpful to increase the depth of the shoulder pad on the side away from the chinrest.

Adding depth to the shoulder pad is an option when the angle of the violin is correct but a gap exists between the existing pad and the student's body.

A simple way to fortify a shoulder pad:
sponge pieces and rubber bands.

In the above photo, the angle of the violin is too great, even though the jaw is in the chinrest. This great an angle impedes the ability of the bow arm to reach the E string and puts strain on the neck.

The additional padding on the right side of the shoulder pad creates a more beneficial angle for the violin, and allows easier access to the E string.

Teachers need to create a framework around the instrument that will allow the student to play without stress. This takes constant vigilance over many years. The unfortunate thing is that as the student grows, the set-up will have to change.

A small ball which balances between the D and G strings demonstrates Paul Rolland's method of determining the proper angle of the violin. The shoulder rest can be padded so the violin sits comfortably in this position, as shown in the above photo. [Rolland, 1974, p 71]

 From a personal point of view, when a student comes into the studio with brand new shoes that look ridiculously large, or with old pants two or three inches too short (each indicating that the student is growing), it's time to carefully assess the set-up of the violin.

One of the things that has amused and baffled me over the years is the random way in which students seem to grow. Sometimes they just get tall and skinny, other times, they get thick with broad shoulders, long arms and disproportionate feet and hands before shooting up. Sometimes little sloped shoulders stay little and sloped, but are attached to a six-foot frame, and other times, little sloped shoulders straighten out and make a rather nice platform for the instrument. Whichever way a student grows, it is our responsibility to watch carefully over the years and adjust the instrument according to the body playing it.

Teachers need to get in the habit of doing a visual sweep of the entire body of the student, including the neck and shoulders (which should be down and back in their natural position), each lesson, for as long as teacher and student are together.

Things to think about ...

1. Create your own plumb bob using 5 feet of heavy string with an object tied at the end. (I used a large steel bolt from a hardware store.)

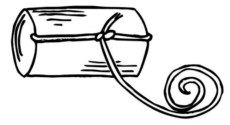

Looking at the figure in Lynn Medoff's article (page 14), hold the string at the level of the ear of your students and align their bodies: ear, shoulder, middle of pelvis, back of knees, and ankle. Do this –

   • without their violins,

   • with their violins and bows, and

   • while playing...have them play a portion of something that they know, stopping and freezing their position when you clap.

   Be sure to check that the backs of the shoulders do not extend beyond their buttocks.

2. Take photos of your students in all three of the above conditions (i.e., with and without violins and in the "frozen" position, and during playing). Do this with at least five subjects of various ages. Write a short description of what you discovered accompanying each set of photographs

3. Imagine the plumb bob being suspended from the right scapula of each of your students. If it hangs free of the buttocks, you may wish to re-evaluate that particular student's posture, as this posture may indicate sway-back, or lordosis, of the spine..

Principles Two and Three...

Range of Motion and Movement

Mid-position in the Range of Motion is Usually Optimal, and Movement Reduces/Eliminates Tension:

These are presented together because one impacts and influences the other.

Principle II: Active range of motion refers to the greatest possible motion produced by muscle contractions.

Principle III: The most desirable movements are those which are near the middle of the range of motion. [Wilson & Roehmann, 1992, p 510; Wolkomir, 1994]

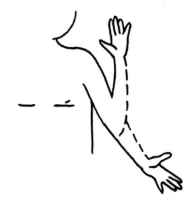

Full active range of motion produced by contractions of biceps and triceps muscles.

These two principles translate into violin playing in critical ways: the obvious one is that teachers need to carefully observe and evaluate the postures and movements of their students EACH lesson. Knowing what to look for, however, can be confusing and challenging to teachers who have never analyzed movement patterns or considered the effects of static tension on playing.

Most of us know that muscles are usually arranged in pairs around skeletal joints. The knee and elbow are examples of this type of joint. When one muscle contracts, the other releases, producing movement toward the contracted muscle. Let's look at drawings of the upper arm.

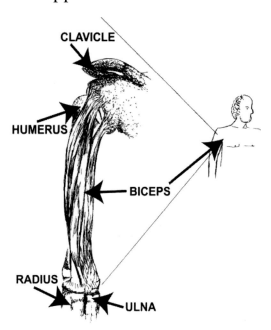

Front of arm.
When the biceps muscle contracts, the triceps elongates, or stretches, to allow the forearm to bend upward toward the contracted muscles.

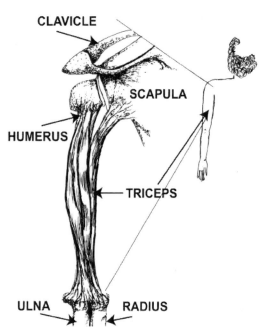

Back of arm.
The triceps muscle is located on the back of the arm. When it contracts, the biceps elongates, or stretches, to allow the forearm to move back into a straight arm.

 Biceps and triceps are examples of muscle pairs that are restricted to hinge joints, or bones that can be moved in one plane. Movements around joints with more than one axis are more complicated, e.g., the shoulder and neck, and the spine.

No matter what type of joint we consider, the body is designed for movement. Violinists are not exempt. "Whether standing or sitting, the violinist does not need to lock a single muscle in the body. Power and support do not come from a held position. They come from a balanced skeleton that is constantly re-balanced by muscles in flow. The skeleton supports the musculature instead of the muscles locking to support the skeleton." [Stein, 2000]

Carla Hannaford, in her wonderful little book, Smart Moves, also states it beautifully, "The more closely we consider the elaborate interplay of brain and body, the more clearly one compelling theme emerges: movement is essential to learning." [Hannaford, 1995, p 96]

Let's see how these principles can be applied in the violin studio.

The Left Arm:

With the violin in playing position, swing the left elbow back and forth as far as it will comfortably go in each direction. This is an easy way to establish active range of motion.

Left elbow's active range of motion for this student.

Finding the approximate center of the arch produced by the swinging elbow establishes where the middle of the range of motion exists.

Middle range of motion.

The voluntary muscles paired around joints of the skeleton are much like healthy heart muscles which contract and relax themselves in synchronous rhythm for many years. As long as they can move freely and in balance with each other, they usually function well. Think of what would happen to the heart if all its muscles were to stay contracted for long periods of time, or if its muscles were constantly co-contracting or pulling against each other simultaneously. Obviously, the outcome would not be positive for the person, or the heart.

If we think of the skeletal muscles in the same way, it becomes apparent that any joint that is locked, or immovable, is risking injury to the muscles, joint, tendons and/or ligaments that support it. So how does this translate to our teaching? The answer is to watch the left elbow and make sure it is in constant motion. I do not mean "thrashing around under the violin" motion. I mean an elbow that is light and ready to center the fingers over whichever string is being played.

The elbow has centered the fingers over the G string, illustrating the "G level" of the left arm. Notice that the elbow is toward the right side of its active range of motion.

"D level"   "A level"   "E level"

As the fingers are centered over successively higher strings, the elbow moves more and more to the student's left.

Teaching beginning students to swing the elbow just enough to center the fingers over the string being played is not difficult, especially if they are told right from the beginning what to do, how to do it, and what to look for.

Activities That Teach Left Elbow Movement

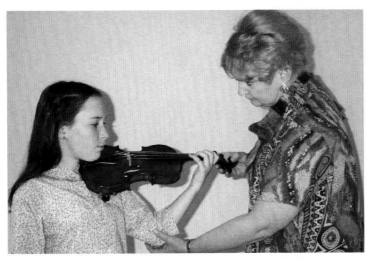

1 The teacher can hold the elbow of the student and move it from side to side.

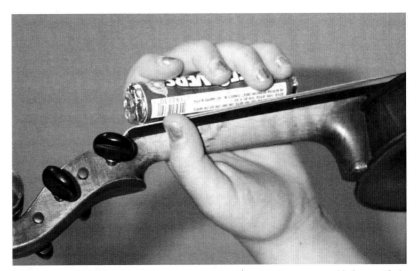

2 Put a Life Saver (Tootsie Roll for small hands) in the curled fingers of the student's left hand. Have them "center" the candy roll over each string by moving the elbow appropriately.

...more

Activities That Teach Left Elbow Movement

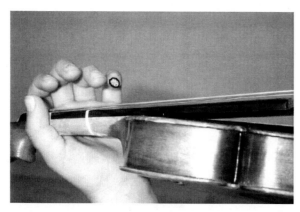

3 Make a small dot (or use a mini-sticker) on the end of the little finger. Have student tap the dot on the E string. Do the same tapping movement on the other strings. Be sure to keep the fourth finger curved and separate from the third finger. If the student always hits the dot or sticker **IN EXACTLY THE SAME PLACE**, the elbow must move under the violin, as the finger centers itself over each new string.

4 The most used technique I have seen to develop the movement of the left elbow is plucking the strings with the little finger of the left hand. If the student keeps the finger curved and soft, the elbow **MUST** move to center the finger over each string. The critical thing here is that the little finger is curved and not thrust away from the other fingers. This posture keeps the pinky and the other fingers in their mid-range of motion.

In the activities below, ✳ indicates two things:

a. the bow stops
b. the left elbow moves to center the fingers over the "new" string.

5 When my own students reach "Song of the Wind" in Book One of the Suzuki Violin School, the left elbow must move to center the fingers over the strings in the passage below. The bow must stop while the elbow centers the fingers over the string to be played. The most critical movement here is the swinging of the elbow AWAY from the student's body BEFORE the A (third finger on the E string) is played:

 I require beginning students to stop playing and move the elbow BEFORE changing strings in early etudes and pieces. This is a critical teaching point in Activity #5 (above) because movements away from the body are more uncomfortable than movements toward it. In this example, the right elbow must also change levels during the bow stop.

6 In "Long, Long Ago" from Book One of the Suzuki Violin School, students stop their bows BEFORE playing on the D string. During the stop, the elbow moves to center the fingers on the D level. After these left hand tasks are completed, the bow can play. Students must also stop their bows and move the elbow back to the A level as soon as they have played the two notes on the D string:

Another issue closely related to this discussion, and already mentioned, is that movement toward the body (adduction) is easier and more accurate than movement away from the body (abduction). This phenomenon is part of the reason students usually have less difficulty shifting up (which brings the arm closer to the body). Conversely, shifting down, or away from the body, is more difficult, and usually takes longer to refine. This also helps explain three phenomena associated with the left arm:

1. left elbow movement toward the student's body is relatively easy,

2. left elbow movement away from the student's body is often uncomfortable for students and overlooked by teachers, and

3. students tend to "lock" their left elbows too far to the right.

Of course, another reason is that teachers might want the elbow further to the right because it WAS considered 'good' posture in the past. As a youngster, I was taught that I should ALWAYS be able to look down and see my left elbow - no matter what string I was on and no matter what position I was in. Of course, in light of the information we now have about how the human body works, these ideas would have to be seriously questioned today.

If we consider the movements of the left elbow in more advanced repertoire, these principles still apply.

From Book One of the Suzuki Violin School, Bach's Minuet 2 gives the left elbow a chance for a real workout for the beginning student.

From Book Four in the Suzuki Violin School, Concerto No. 5, 1st Movement, by Seitz.

The last movement of the Mendelssohn Concerto (in E minor) is filled with passages requiring centering movements of the left elbow. In fact, examples are limitless. It is up to each teacher to analyze, play and re-analyze the repertoire he/she teaches for passages requiring these kinds of left elbow movements. Finally, we must observe the students and make certain their elbows are centered in their ranges of motion, and are moving enough to center the fingers over the appropriate strings all the time they are playing.

 If students have been taught at the beginning to stop the bow in order for the left elbow to move to the new string, their bodies will learn a natural rhythm for the two actions. By the time they have reached advanced repertoire, the movements are small, unconscious, fluid, and simultaneous.

The Left Hand and Wrist:

The same principles apply to both wrists. We must be aware that wrists move in more than a single plane. Let's consider two movements: up and down and back and forth.

First, establish active range of motion for up and down motions, then notice the mid-range of motion.

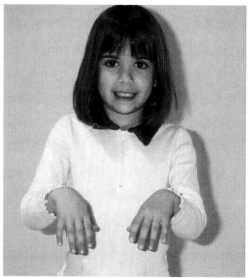

The above photos show the range of motion up and down
for this student's wrists.

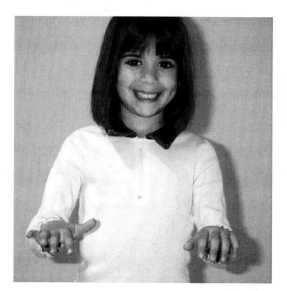
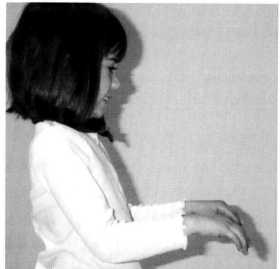

These photos show the student in the middle of the
up/down range of motion.

The "pancake wrist" hampers technical progress and carries the risk of stress because the hand and wrist are locked and are not in the middle of the wrist's range of motion.

Commonly called the "pancake" wrist, this position, when maintained, not only impedes intonation, shifting and vibrato, but also puts the student at risk for injury.

The basic set-up of the left hand and wrist changes according to their size and proportion. Since we are trying to form each hand in such a way that fingers and wrists are in the middle of their respective active ranges of motion, we must consider more than "a straight" left wrist. For example, we must be aware of the length of the little finger in respect to the rest of the hand. Violinists risk injury by constantly thrusting the little finger too far away from the hand or by using too much force. Both put the little finger at an extreme of its range of motion. We must think about setting the hand up in a way that is more user-friendly to the little finger.

Take a close look at yourself and your students. Quietly note what the little finger is doing each time it plays. If it is straight and thrust out from the rest of the hand, you might want to begin a re-training regime, which includes both the little finger, forearm, wrist and hand.

These photos show the same hand from both sides:

Notice the tension in the little finger: the hand is set low on the neck of the violin, which forces the joints of the finger to be rigid. The locked pinky, in turn, promotes flexation of the left wrist.

The tension the extended wrist puts on the thumb is apparent from this view.

Bringing the little finger into its own mid-range of motion will help to reduce trauma by returning it to a curved, natural position. Raising the height of the left hand on the neck of the violin will often serve to reduce tension in the little finger, thus reducing the need or tendency for the wrist to flex. I have found it useful to use the **LITTLE FINGER** as the gauge by which the height of the left hand is initially set.

This photo shows a position that is friendlier to the body and allows for slight movement to accommodate finger patterns outside of the basic octave frame and/or shifting.

Measuring the depth of the hand on the neck of the violin has traditionally been done between the thumb and the base of the first finger. While this works for most hands, it is a clear disadvantage to a small hand, a hand with shorter fingers, or a very short little finger. Measuring from the base of the little finger helps reduce these disadvantages.

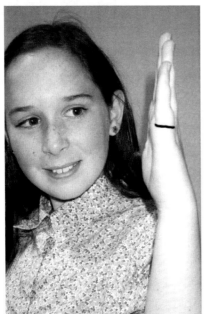

Drawing a line at the base of the little finger (where it meets the palm of the hand) gives a good visual clue that determines the depth of the hand on the violin.

The hand needs to be placed next to the instrument in such a way that the little finger can fall from its base joint in a natural, curved position.

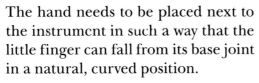

The pinky-side of the hand is slowest to develop and is the weakest. For these reasons, it is important to delay the use of the fourth finger with very young students until it can be precisely controlled. Teachers can help develop the musculature of the hands of their students by encouraging them to pick up objects between the thumb and ring finger and between the thumb and pinky, or by passing a tissue back and forth between the thumb and a round pinky, or by newspaper crunching. All these are described below and on the next page.

Activities for Developing the Little Finger (Pinky) Side of the Left Hand:

1 In this photo, the student is picking up small objects from the floor and dropping them in the dish. She is challenged to pick the object up between her thumb and little finger, which she must keep rounded and soft.

2 Passing a tissue around the circle. As with Activity #1, make sure the pinky and thumb are curved. (Try this with each finger of each hand – always soft and curved.)

...more
Activities for Developing the Left Hand

 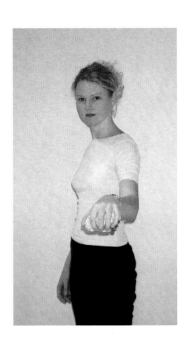

3 Perhaps the best activity I have found for developing the muscles of the hand was shared with me by a studio parent who is a physical therapist. She said that therapists at the University of New Mexico Hospital employ "newspaper crunching" to strengthen hands and promote flexibility. The idea is to take a full sheet of newspaper (for an adult or adolescent) in one hand and begin crunching it until it is completely contained in the palm of the hand. Younger students should use half a sheet and really young students, a quarter sheet. The only rule is that you may not touch anything else while crunching the newspaper, and you may not use the other hand at all. To balance this "workout," do it with both hands.

 The above photos show the hand hanging below the wrist. In actuality, however, the hand, wrist and fingers will all be actively moving throughout their respective active ranges of motion.

The Right Hand and Wrist:

Now, let's apply these principles to the right hand and wrist.

The bow arm should be flat from the knuckles of the hand to the elbow when the bow arm is in its neutral position, sometimes called the "square" of the arm.

The "square" of the arm (home position) is where the wrist and elbow are in the middle of their ranges of motion. Notice the 90° angles between bow and hand, and forearm and upper arm.

In this neutral position, the bow arm can raise or lower to contact any of the four strings, which benefits the shoulder joint by keeping it in motion. The mid-range of the shoulder joint will be on, or about the A or D level.

Also from this neutral position, all strokes and string crossings can be developed in such a way as to minimize static tensions in the right arm and hand. For example, it is useful to insist that the arm be on the E level WHENEVER THE STUDENT IS PLAYING ON THE E STRING. This simple requirement helps insure that the shoulder hinge does not remain static. When the bow arm is suspended for long periods of time, the muscles in the shoulder (rotator cuff muscles), which are small in comparison to the deltoid and pectoralis major, can be easily stressed or injured. [Thompson & Floyd, 1998, p 40]

Like the left elbow, the right arm also has "levels" appropriate to the string being played. This photo shows the right arm on the E string.

Bow arm on the G string.

The shoulder is a ball and socket joint that has a large range of motion. The four little muscles that make it move, however, do not have much room to work. For this reason, there is a natural lubricating tissue, called a bursa, which lies on the tendons at the end of these little muscles. This lubrication usually allows the tendons to glide smoothly between the bone at the top of the shoulder, the acromion, and the top, or head, of the humerus.

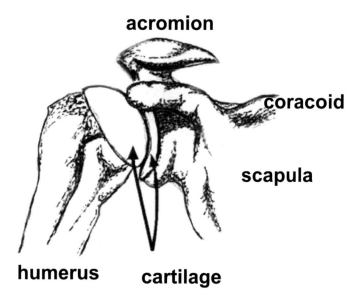

Bones in the rotator cuff area of the shoulder joint.

View from the side of the body. The tendons of the four little muscles surround the top, back and front of the joint like a "cuff".

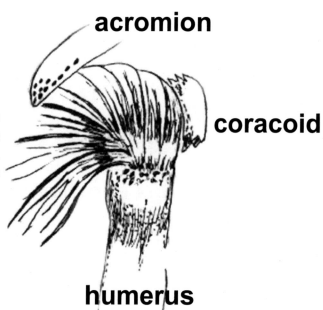

The name "rotator cuff" suggests a lot about the anatomy of this small area of the shoulder. The "cuff" part refers to the tendonous ends of four small muscles which surround the top of the shoulder joint like the cuff of a shirt-sleeve surrounds our wrist. These little muscles originate on the scapula, or shoulder blade, and pull on the upper end (head) of the humerus. When the muscles pull, the tendons which attach them to the humerus "rotate" the shoulder.

Injury to the tendons can be the result of three things, THE LAST OF WHICH IS OF PARTICULAR INTEREST TO VIOLINISTS: 1. Some people have inherited a smaller than usual space in which these tendons can work; 2. Injury can result from repetitive and stressful activities that require elevation of the arm, such as lifting, swimming, throwing a ball, etc.; and 3. IMBALANCE OF THE SHOULDER JOINT, WHICH CAN CAUSE THE SHOULDER TO MOVE FORWARD, IN A LOCKED POSITION, FOR EXTENDED PERIODS OF TIME. (emphasis added) [S.C.O.I., Rotator Cuff Disease/Impingement]

Again, drawing on my experience as a Suzuki specialist, there are three "watch point" pieces which help my students and me determine how well the bow arm is being trained. Twinkle is always taught with the arm on the E level, but other early training opportunities for beginners are:

1 "O Come Little Children" (Suzuki Violin School, Book One). Check that the right arm is on the E level each time the student plays on the E string.

2 "May Song" (Suzuki Violin School, Book One). Watch the E level of the bow arm carefully here.

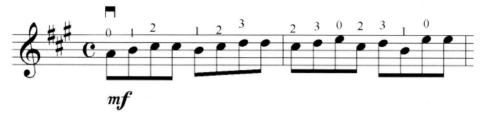

3 "Perpetual Motion" (Suzuki Violin School, Book One). Use this piece as a quiet way to assess how well the bow arm is learning. Watch for E level EACH TIME THE STUDENT IS PLAYING ON THE E STRING. After you have made a personal judgement, let the student know how well his/her bow arm is doing. If the student is having difficulty, have them stop the bow, move the arm to the E level, then play.

These are examples of beginning pieces in which the E level of the right arm must be watched constantly. The truth is, however, that this (E level of the bow arm) must be constantly watched – no matter how advanced the student. This can be frustrating for teachers and students because it is especially easy for young players with little skinny arms to suspend the right elbow for long periods during practice. If the body adopts this posture because of many hours of incorrect practice, it has the potential to be injurious, especially later on when the child grows and the weight of the arm increases. However, the bow arm doesn't know this. It is just trying to fulfill the musical demands being placed on it. This puts added responsibility on the teacher.

String crossings using the elbow, wrist and/or fingers all represent other types of up/down motions, and can be accomplished within the parameters of these two principles, i.e., stay in the middle range of motion and keep moving. For example, I teach a forearm string crossing using the elbow hinge.

This photo shows "home position," or the square of the arm.

The forearm string crossing is an early skill. It can be used any time the music requires the student to change to a lower string for only a note or two.

The raised forearm demonstrates a forearm crossing.

The following are musical examples taken from the Suzuki Violin School, Book One, where a forearm crossing might be used:

In Etude, above, the notes on the D string may be reached using a forearm crossing.

The first two measures of Minuet 2, above, are more complicated because the student must control the bow arm quickly and accurately.

To simplify, have the student play the same passage without the left hand, stopping and adjusting the bow arm for each string, but reaching the fifth note (open A) with a forearm crossing.

As the larger muscles of the student become trained and are moving easily, the smaller muscles of the hand and wrist can come into training with a hand-up string crossing.

This type of string crossing, referred to here as a hand up string crossing, may be used for faster or repeated string crossing requirements.

It is important that the student practice a hand-up crossing with a small movement, which stays close to both strings. The bow stick should remain quiet and "on top of the hair" throughout the entire crossing (up and back down). Again, the hand is up only slightly for the crossing and returns to its neutral position, which is in its mid-range of motion.

Another type of string crossing is a finger crossing.

Here, the flexible round fingers (in the middle of their respective ranges of motion) allow for another kind of string crossing using primarily the fingers.

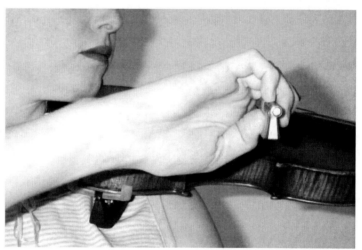

Deeply curved fingers raise the bow slightly for a "finger crossing."

All string crossings are directed in an upward motion, and all return to the neutral position of the activated joint. The constant, however, no matter which string crossing is employed, is the E level of the right elbow whenever the student plays on the E string.

Back and Forth Movements of the Wrists:

Establish range of motion for back and forth movements of the wrist. The photos below show active back and forth ranges of motion for two right wrists.

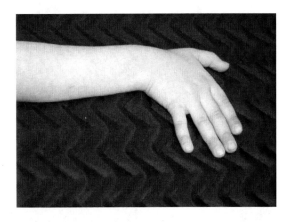

When the hand turns itself toward the ulna (a bone in the forearm) it is called ULNAR DEVIATION.

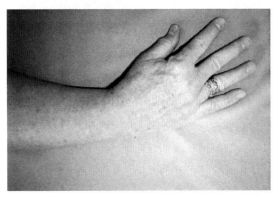

When the hand turns itself toward the radius (another bone in the forearm) it is called RADIAL DEVIATION.

A simple way to think of the optimal positions of the hands in this "back and forth" range of motion is to think of a straight line that runs from the base of the fingers to the elbows of both arms. This imaginary line keeps the wrists in their mid-range of motion, which is their most desirable position.

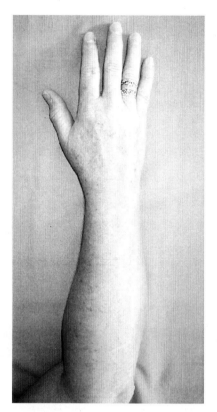 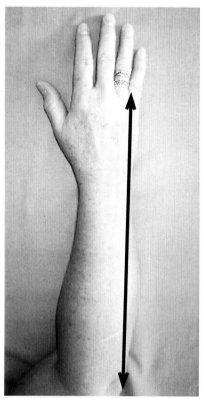

These photos illustrate a wrist without ulnar or radial deviation. By visualizing an arrow, or straight line, as shown on the right, it is easier for teachers to identify the slightest deviation of the wrist in either direction.

If either hand is allowed to repeatedly go into ulnar or radial deviation, the student is at risk for injury. Achieving mid-range of motion, or straight wrists, in both right and left hands can be time-consuming and sometimes a bit experimental because each set of hands and arms is different.

The student below is demonstrating mid-range of back and forth movement of both wrists.

In the above photos, note the straight line from knuckles to elbow in both arms – a good representation of "home position" for the violinist.

Compare the above photos with the photos below:

These photos show ulnar deviation in both hands.

In general, it seems that I have been able to reduce the teaching of both hands down to a few thoughts:

1. Reducing ulnar or radial deviation in the left hand:

Back in the days when I was using binoculars, I also noticed that both the right and left wrists and forearms of great players were straight. In experimenting with this over many years, I began to notice that the callouses of these players were consistently slightly on the outside, or "thumb" side of their first fingers.

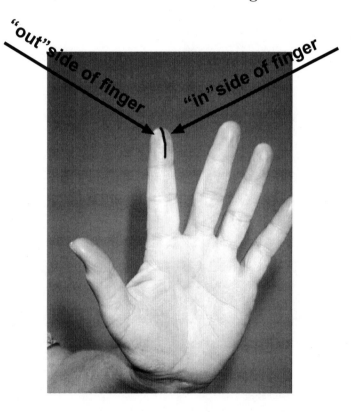

A line drawn down the middle of the student's left first finger creates an "out"side half (thumb side) and an "in"side half (finger side).

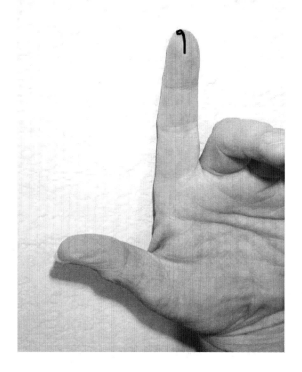

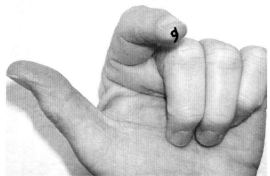

The left hand, showing the relationship of dot-to-line (left photo), and end of finger, showing relationship of line-to-dot (above photo). Please note that the dot touches the line.

If students are allowed, or become accustomed, to touching the string on the finger side, or "in" side of their first fingers, it creates difficulties for them, including ulnar deviation, and what John Kendall refers to as "knock-kneed knuckles."

 I have shared this idea of placing the first finger slightly on the outside, or thumb side, with several teachers, only to be dismayed by hearing them tell students to play on the "corner" of the finger! This position, for most hands, can create other tensions. A better alternative might be to draw the line down the center of the student's finger and then draw a small dot touching the line on its outside edge, as shown in the above photos.

When first finger touches the string on the "in"side of the finger, it invites "knock-kneed knuckles" and ulnar deviation. The angle of the first finger is such that it is driven into the second finger, virtually locking them together and reducing mobility in both. Note also that the fourth finger has no access to the string in this position.

When first finger touches the string SLIGHTLY ON THE "OUT"SIDE, OR THUMB SIDE, it helps reduce the tendency for ulnar deviation. Note that the fourth finger is also curved and accessible to the string. I refer to this as "Home Position" for the left hand.

Establishing home position for the left hand requires the hand to be set high enough for all the fingers to remain curved over the fingerboard with the first finger touching the string slightly on the thumb side and the left elbow "hanging" in its mid-range of motion beneath the violin.

String changes can then be accomplished by a swinging movement of the left elbow. Each swinging movement centers the fingers over the appropriate string. This type of training of the left hand and arm virtually eliminates ulnar deviation. (A discussion and photos of this swinging movement of the left elbow may be found on pages 33-35.)

2. Reducing ulnar or radial deviation in the right hand:

This is where the teacher might want to do a bit of experimenting with the student's bow arm. The trick is to get the bow to the frog without back and forth movement of the wrist (ulnar or radial deviation), keeping the right wrist in its mid-range of motion. In other words, keep the same straight line between base of the little finger and elbow that we created in the left hand.

I experimented for a long time with this concept and am currently using the following approach:

FIRST, teach the student to bend the wrist up and down slightly, and tell the student that this movement is not so traumatic. Next, have the student bend his or her wrist back and forth. Tell the student that this movement may be injurious if constantly repeated.

SECOND, help the student go to the frog by lifting the wrist SLIGHTLY upward and "chasing" the tip of the bow with the right elbow. This necessitates movement of the upper arm, or the shoulder.

THIRD, the movement of the upper arm follows the tip of the bow and the elbow. It does not begin to fall down next to the body, which inhibits movement and flexibility at the frog.

FOURTH, as the bow moves toward the frog, the wrist rounds up slightly. Be sure that the line from base of pinky to elbow remains straight and the little finger remains curved and close to the other fingers.

 An easy way to identify ulnar deviation of the wrist is looking for the wrinkles that occur on the outside of the wrist when it is in ulnar deviation.

Home position.

As the bow begins to travel to the frog, raise the wrist very slightly.

As the hand moves closer to the frog, the elbow floats up behind it. This movement is slightly different for each student because of varying length of fingers and arms and their relative proportions to the body. Continue to experiment until the student can go to the frog without even a hint of ulnar deviation.

This type of bow arm training requires all the joints to move (including the shoulder), keeps the joints centered in their mid-range of motion, and eliminates ulnar and radial deviation.

I have jury-rigged student's arms to help me and them recognize and achieve this movement pattern. By attaching two pencils with two rubber bands around the hand and wrist of the student, they can move the wrist up and down slightly, but back and forth movement (ulnar and radial deviation) is uncomfortable. This can be used on either right or left hand.

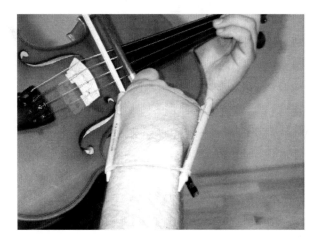

This jury-rigged bow arm helps the student get to the frog without ulnar or radial deviation – a worthy goal for all students.

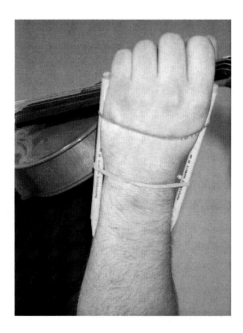

Jury-rigging the left wrist helps the student feel a straight left wrist. This is especially useful when playing simple passages that require the fingers to be centered over more than one or two strings.

Things to think about . . .

1. Violinists' left elbows should be in constant motion, which has at least two benefits:

    a. By centering the fingers over each string, it helps reduce the need to overextend the fingers, especially third and fourth fingers.

    b. Motion reduces static tension.

Do a measure-by-measure analysis of the short excerpts on the following pages, indicating (**BY WRITING BELOW THE STAFF**) where left elbow movement should occur, and in which direction, as such:

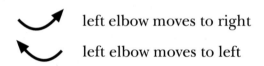

    left elbow moves to right

    left elbow moves to left

2. This chapter addresses several important movements of the right arm: including E level, arm levels for each string, "forearm," "hand up" and "finger" string crossings. Returning to the excerpts on the following pages, do an analysis of right arm and hand positions. Use the following abbreviations (**WRITING BELOW THE STAFF**):

E = E level

HP = home position

HPA = home position on A string (HPD = home position on D string, etc.)

F = forearm crossing

H = hand up crossing

Fi = finger crossing

There is no right way to use string crossings; it is up to each player to decide which fits his/her body best. Usually, the quicker the string crossing, the smaller the muscle. The rationale here is to keep all joints flexible and moving.

The first few measures for both exercises have been done for you:

1 Concerto in G Major, 1st Movement, by Haydn.

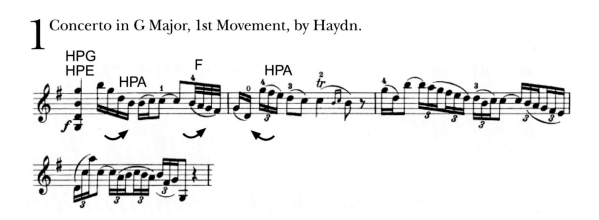

2 Concerto No. 1, 1st Movement, by Accolay.

3 Sonata No. 5, 1st Movement, by Mozart.

4 Concerto in E Minor, 3rd Movement, by Mendelssohn.

5 Partita No. 3, by J.S. Bach.

6 Sonata for Solo Violin, 2nd Movement, 2nd Variation, Opus 115, by Prokofieff.

Principle Number Four...

Muscles Have Memory:

How movement patterns are acquired

Voluntary muscles move because they receive directives to do so. They do not know that certain movement patterns and static tensions that are being "tried out" or used during the learning process might be repeated tens of thousands of times. This can be thought of as a "top-down" dialogue between the mind and the muscles. What the mind wants, the muscles do.

An example of "top-down" dialogue.

During the early stages of learning, muscle combinations, tensions and releases are under conscious control and continue to change and re-configure themselves according to what the mind has ordered. In other words, a perceptual mandate creates a mental template. The muscles, through trial and error, attempt to achieve what the mind has conceived, or come as close to the template as possible. As the mind receives knowledge of results, subsequent movements are changed and refined until the desired degree of accuracy is achieved. [Dickinson. 1985, p 209]

Closed-Loop Movements:

Muscles begin learning by trying out various combinations of tensions and releases with selected muscles, or parts of muscles, until the resulting movement fits as closely as possible to the brain's idea.

It is during these early stages of acquisition that teachers need to be particularly aware of what the student's body is doing. The reason: THE MUSCLES ARE MALLEABLE IN THEIR EARLY EFFORTS. They have not yet adopted an automatic response pattern, which makes it relatively easy to make changes and/or fine adjustments.

This acquisition stage presents an opportunity and a challenge for teachers to carefully observe all aspects of the student's movements, including angles, tensions and postures and to make corrections for as long as it takes for the muscles to become accustomed to productive, non-injurious movements and postures. It is also extremely important that the brain of the student be able to direct the muscles to these ends. The student, therefore, must know enough to consciously direct his/her own muscles in movements that match a mental template which has been carefully constructed by the teacher - a huge chunk of the early learning experience, therefore, focuses on training the body, which supports the teaching approach postulated in the "Introduction" of this book.

If musical outcomes are the only stimulus which drives the muscles, they may or may not adopt beneficial movement patterns, which leaves the student at risk. Furthermore, dividing the limited resources of students' working memory between new, sometimes uncomfortable, movements AND musical outcomes (rhythm, meter, phrasing) may not be possible at this time.

In addition to the "top-down" model, early stages of muscle acquisition can also be thought to have a circular pattern, with each repetition producing slight refinements and/or variations.

This type of movement is commonly called "closed loop" movement, and although my diagram is not an exact duplication, it harkens back to the original model, *Adams' Closed-Loop Theory*. [Dickinson. 1985, p 212]

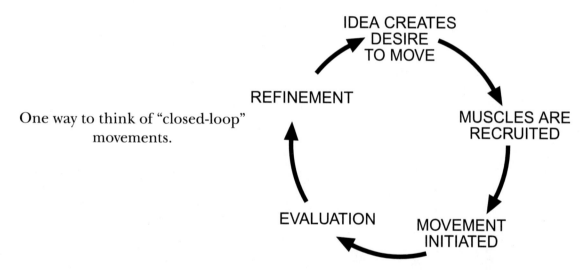

One way to think of "closed-loop" movements.

Although there have been flaws found in the closed-loop theory, criticism has centered on Adams' inadequate explanation of highly-skilled, or automatic movements and on how he described storage and retrieval of the perceptual trace. I have yet to read a researcher who doesn't agree that muscles initially learn and refine their patterns via repetition. They learn best what they have done the most, and the more they repeat a movement, the better they know it and can reproduce it.

The closed-loop diagram is presented here specifically because of its usefulness to teachers. **DURING THIS STAGE, STUDENTS ARE**

AWARE OF WHAT THEY ARE DOING AND CAN MAKE CHANGES MORE EASILY, and teachers can make certain that fingers, arms, wrists and body are moving in user-friendly ways, so those movements are the ones being acquired.

Another characteristic of this stage of acquisition is that when refinements or changes are made, the whole cycle begins again. In other words, when we require a student to avoid ulnar deviation by correct placement of the first finger on the string (or keeping fourth finger curved over the fingerboard, or any other common problem), he/she must begin the cycle anew – with a different "idea to move." Now the idea to move is loaded with "place first finger on the 'out' side or 'thumb' side," which slightly changes the entire movement. The longer this "refinement" (students call it "nagging") goes on, the longer the movement remains under the student's conscious control and the greater the muscle control – a remarkable teaching tool in itself!

This is a critical time for both teacher and student. Let's assume a movement has been successful for a lesson or two. As long as the student keeps the movement under conscious control (i.e. working memory), it seems to work, so the natural tendency for both teacher and student might be to go on with something else. The trouble: The student's body has not yet adopted the movement. As soon as his/her working memory is redirected, it will reacquire the comfortable and most used way of moving. For this reason, it is the responsibility of the teacher to monitor the movement and remind the student for months, or years, whatever it takes. (A more complete description of this phenomenon is in the next chapter on Proactive Interference.)

Ballistic Movements:

Perhaps a familiar example of ballistic movement is throwing a ball. The speed and trajectory are planned in advance, but once the ball is thrown, there is no way to correct for faulty planning.

The violinist's need to repeat passages over and over is driven by two factors, 1. the demands of the music, and 2. to produce movement patterns that are so automatic that they become virtually unconscious.

Movements that are largely unconscious are referred to as *ballistic movements*, which have some unique characteristics. First, all the "details of the movement must have been completely worked out in advance, in a lengthy trial and error process, so that the movement can be executed when it is called for with absolute accuracy, each and every time, in a nearly automatic way. This means that the brain, or motor control system, must issue in advance of the move an ordered series of command signals that specify what the muscles involved must do, from start to finish, **BEFORE THE MOVEMENT ITSELF ACTUALLY BEGINS**... Another equally significant feature is the striking change in muscle responsiveness that occurs in this condition. The physical fluidity which a performer enjoys when he or she is 'on', or is playing 'unconsciously,' almost certainly stems from a marked shift in the physiologic behavior of muscles coming under ballistic control." (emphasis added) [Wilson, 1986, pp 50 - 51]

Ballistic movement might be diagrammed as follows

desire to move → **muscles are recruited and directed** → **movement completed**

There are many ways for a finger to depress a string: contact points may change, hinges can be deeply curved, or straight, or anything in between, and force can vary from a feather touch to heavy pounding. If string teachers concentrate too much on "the music" and leave the multitude of options available to the body producing it to chance, there almost certainly will be some of what Frank Wilson calls chaotic ballistic movement: "The final misery...may simply reflect the paradoxical consequence of the distraught musician practicing in an abnormal condition, thereby effectively locking in an end-stage chaotic ballistic program that can degrade further each time the movement is attempted again." [Wilson & Roehmann, 1992, p 515]

The mandate for violinists, and teachers in particular, is that analysis of how students use their bodies during lessons and performance is not just for "beginners," but is an on-going and essential component of the teaching process, especially during the acquisition stage. Teachers who educate their students to wisely direct their own movements, thereby lingering in closed-loop phases of movement acquisition put themselves and their students in a safer and more productive learning environment.

Things to think about . . .

1. Here is an activity that is extremely useful to the violin teacher. Prepare the following piece holding the violin backward, or on the right shoulder. Require yourself to maintain good posture, bow hold and octave frame of the right hand - all of which are comfortable and automatic on the other side.

Swedish Lullaby sung to me by my mother.

As simple as this little song is, when we attempt to play it with the violin on the opposite shoulder, it helps us appreciate how strong muscle memory is, and what our students are experiencing. Attending to the body becomes as big a hurdle as playing the piece – a real-life example of how limited Working Memory resources are.

Principle Number Five...

Proactive Interference:

Its Issues and Effects

This discussion augments and clarifies the previous chapter's short introduction to muscle memory.

Proactive interference refers to a situation in which the body has learned a posture or movement well, and then has to change, or re-configure itself. As previously mentioned, the mind-body duo wants to economize, thereby conserving the work load on both. As movements or postures are repeated over and over, they become more and more automatic, they begin to feel comfortable and eventually become almost unconscious, which reduces the load on working memory. An example of such a well-learned posture is your bow hold. Just for fun, pick up a bow, pencil, pen or anything else readily available and make a bow hold. You probably didn't have to think about each separate finger, your thumb or the amount of tension in each, or where the bow hold should be placed on the bow (if you are using one). You thought "bow hold" and there it was! What would happen if you were told to change your bow hold? You would have to consciously re-examine and evaluate each separate finger, the thumb and the amount of tension as you directed muscles to comply with the new directions. The frustrating reality is that the moment you stop consciously monitoring EACH COMPONENT of the "new" bow hold, it will happily return to the comfortable one it knows. This is an example of proactive interference.

Researchers noted that in a variety of settings, proactive interference disrupted or delayed the learning of a desired movement or movement sequence. [Dickinson, 1985, pp 221-223; Wulf & Schmidt, 1994, p 360; Lee & Magill, 1985, pp 23-41]

Diagramed, it looks like this:

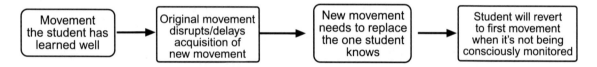

Helen Higa, one of the reviewers of this manuscript, suggested I insert an Alexander model here, another way of thinking about the effects of proactive interference.

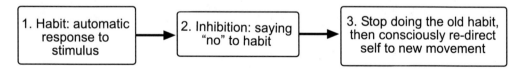

Some of the most compelling literature does not directly concern itself with proactive interference, but with the nature of skilled acquisition. These hypotheses, even though differing somewhat from one another, also support our discussion about closed-loop movement and proactive interference.

I would like to share two of these hypotheses:

Fitt's Stages:

1ST STAGE: [Cognitive] The learner seeks to understand the nature of the problem and initiates practice on single components. There is little or no integration into other skills or situations. Depending on the past experience of the learner, this stage can be one of extremely slow growth or rapid growth. Each component is under voluntary control.

Using our previous example of the bowhold: the student might spend a long time trying to control the bent thumb, or the placement of each of the fingers on the stick, or the amount of tension necessary to hold and support the bow, but not so much as to cause inflexibility of the fingers.

2ND STAGE: [Associative] During this stage, the skill is smoothed out and motor strategies are refined. Rudimentary components are integrated and whole-task practice may begin. The skill is still under voluntary control.

In this stage, the student has control over most aspects of the bowhold, but is still struggling with components. During this stage, teachers find themselves nagging students, "Bend your thumb, or pinky" or "Don't wrap the first finger around the bow" or "Keep a light touch." The student may be grappling, but most of the components are beginning to feel comfortable and can be used in elementary bow strokes and string crossings without further disruption.

3RD STAGE: [Autonomous] This stage occupies the longest practice time as highly skilled performance slowly develops. Continual repetitions transfers control from voluntary to automatic control.

Without thinking of individual components of the basic bowhold, the student can begin to develop more advanced bow strokes and string crossings.

[Norman. 1987, pp 84-86]

Another description of skill acquisition was proposed by Anderson, who felt that Fitt's stages were purely descriptive, but not explanatory:

Anderson's Stages:

1st stage: [Declarative]: Learner receives information which is integrated into the past procedures already in his/her long term motor memory. This combination of "new" and "old" generates an approximation of the skill, or a component of the skill.

The student knows that fingers are supposed to be curved, separate and soft. The teacher has likened the bowhold to the natural position of the hand when it is at rest at the student's side. The student knows what it feels like for the hand to be at rest and tries to duplicate the feeling and posture when holding the bow.

2nd stage: [Knowledge Compilation] Practice causes this basic knowledge to gradually convert from declarative knowledge (knowing that...) to procedural knowledge (knowing how...). This stage consists of sets of production rules which link input (the brain's idea) to output (the muscle's response).

The fingers begin to assume the correct position without mental directives about each component. The fingers know what position they are to be in and each finds its relative place. The student is aware of what the fingers are supposed to be doing and is able to monitor each. The danger here is that if Working Memory is overloaded, the resources to monitor the bowhold may be too limited to attend to each individual component, which might occur when all available capacity is necessary to play too challenging a piece of music.

3rd stage: [Procedural] Practice refines and strengthens procedures, which can be generalized to similar tasks.

The bowhold is stable enough for the student to begin to experiment with different touches and balances required for different strokes. For example, a shallower bowhold with even lighter fingers might serve for expressive playing, the little finger might lift for fast passages, etc.

[Norman, 1987, pp 86-88]

Whether we consider Fitt's or Anderson's work, or other descriptive/explanatory processes (e.g., for those of you who may be interested: schema theory, or Rasmussen's paradigm), similarities exist. For example, all show that skill is acquired through simple processes that progress from ideas to movement, which are mastered through repetition.

The applications to teaching are obvious. Most experienced teachers recognize a graduated pattern of acquisition – from elementary components to advanced skills. If this is true, why adopt teaching strategies that necessitate RE-TRAINING of movements or gestures? An excellent question! Let's explore some implications.

Researchers who study movement agree that voluntary movement begins with an idea, which is transmitted to commands, which drive the muscles. As muscles move in repetitive patterns, they begin to feel comfortable and with even more repetitions, will adopt each component of the pattern into a highly learned, automated skill. As I mentioned earlier, muscles do not make a decision about the "best" way to move, they simply try to satisfy the demands made on them. From this point of view, it is clear that it is the cognitive command that determines what the muscles do – for better or worse.

In order for optimal movement patterns to be adopted by our students, the cognitive command must contain two elements: the appropriate musical element (rhythm, pitch, meter, etc.), and the kinesthetic element (how to do it in a non-injurious way). Students must know what they are trying to do musically and must know exactly how to accomplish it with movements and postures that reduce the possibility of trauma to the body.

The issues of proactive interference and how skilled behavior are developed have begun to dominate my teaching, especially for the first several years a student studies. I would like to share with you some of my thoughts:

Proactive Interference - Implications for teachers:

First, linger in the early stages of acquisition:

I used to feel pressure to push students along as quickly as possible, always going to the "next" piece, always pushing for more advanced literature, always pushing for more speed and agility, and always trying to get to music that I ENJOYED PLAYING AND TEACHING.

I also used to think that my students needed to have an aesthetic relationship with music exactly like mine. What I failed to acknowledge was that young students who are physical learners ARE having a fulfilling musical experience and that older beginners WILL have one.

It's a bit like my student nursing days when our charge nurse would exude ecstasy over increased urine output of a sick child. Even though I was interested, it was obvious that her knowledge and years of experience allowed her to have greater understanding and aesthetic response (which it seemed to be) than I. While I was happy the child was improving, I had no comprehension of the potential courses the illness might have taken, or the array of potential treatments. The head nurse and I responded differently according to our individual levels of understanding. Even though the responses were fulfilling to each of us, the difference was in our levels of understanding.

I have begun to accept this same thing in my students. As their experience and technique grow, their response to music has the potential to grow from one of pleasure to one of true aesthetic feelings. From this particular point of view, then, technique facilitates feelingful responses to music.

Every researcher I have read agrees that in the initial stages of learning, movement is under conscious control. This is the critical time for teachers because changes and refinements can be made more easily, AND IF THEY ARE MADE EACH WEEK, THE MOVEMENTS AND POS-TURES HAVE LITTLE OPPORTUNITY TO COME UNDER UNCONSCIOUS CONTROL. This translates into is being able to insist that the body is functioning optimally – both before playing (the set-up of the student) and during playing.

> How long and well we can insist that the body moves beneficially might be the magic key for students to integrate all the components of their technique, and might be the factor in determining later technical development.

There is not one experienced teacher who has not been preparing a student for a performance, concentrating solely on the music, only to discover after-the-fact that things have gone awry with his/her technique. If we give credence to the research, then we should be:

- making corrections immediately,
- giving specific instructions on how the student is to accomplish those corrections,
- continuing to correct until the body has complied, and
- continuing to assess and observe over long periods of time.

Second, teach as closely as possible to what the finished product will be:

For example, Suzuki teachers use an elementary bowhold (I call it "the baby bowhold") for children under the age of five or six years old. Because of limitations in fine motor control, this works well with these students. This research suggests that the baby bowhold be as close to the real bowhold as possible. For example, placing the thumb on both the hair and the frog sets it immediately above where it will eventually sit. If the thumb is placed in the middle of the frog, it has to re-configure itself when progressing to the advanced hold. This might seem like a small thing, but it isn't to the child, the thumb, or the rest of the hand's/finger's relationship to it.

The same principles apply when setting up the left hand. If you carefully watch the hands of professional players, it is obvious that the base of the first finger is not pinching, or locked under the neck of the violin. Rather, there is a straight line from the elbow to the base of the little finger and the base of the first finger is lightly touching, or a paper's width away from the neck of the violin. These, then, become factors in setting up the initial frame of the left hand. Having the student begin by holding the neck of the violin between the thumb and base joint of the first finger and leaving it for weeks at a time teaches those muscles just that, which interferes with shifting and vibrato later on. I have found that even young children can learn to touch the violin lightly without tension in the left hand.

> It is difficult for teachers to see tension in the hands of young children, and for this reason, from the beginning, either my hand, or the hand of their parent should be on their left hands – especially when they are beginning to put fingers down.

I also have students begin with "touch-set" fingers, which are placed independently. The first finger my students learn is the third finger, which has its own tape on the fingerboard, giving the student a visual as to its exact placement. Once the finger is placed in a soft, curved posture on the string, but not depressing it (which might take several weeks), the rest of the hand finds its own place on the neck. In other words, I am using third (and fourth passively) to set the octave frame of the hand, rather than the first finger (which is more difficult to train because it swings horizontally and sits slightly on the thumb side). Once third and second have been placed so they are soft, separate from the other fingers and curved together in an arch (which includes the fourth finger), THEN the first finger finds its place and the thumb places itself where it has no tension. The hand BEGINS in a usable octave frame without grasping or clenching between the base of the first finger and the thumb.

When fingers barely touch the string, but do not move it or depress it, I call it "touching" the string. Fingers two and three (with four above the string and in an arch with the others) practice "touching" the string in their exact spots for as long as it takes for them to begin to be consistent in their efforts to come down on the string. The bow is not used here and the string is not depressed, and either my hand or the hand of the parent is always on the hand of the child to insure that there is no tension developing in the left hand. When this movement is stable and predictable, then the student begins to "set" the string on the fingerboard. Only enough pressure for the string to touch the fingerboard is necessary. Still no bow (which could overload working memory) and still the parent's or my hand is feeling for tension in the hand of the student. The student would now be ready to play his/her first piece using third finger on either A or E strings, or both. Second finger is quick to follow. Now the student can play a piece using second and third fingers on both E and A strings. In the meantime, we are preparing first finger by placing it slightly on the thumb side and teaching it to swing from the base-joint of the hand and watching that the base of the finger is free from clutching the neck of the violin. When this action is consistent, the bow may be added for first finger. Now the child is ready for pieces incorporating all three fingers. Still, the parent's hand, or mine, is always on the child's left hand.

This may seem like a tedious approach for teachers who are accustomed to moving beginners along at a faster pace, but the rewards are in the future. I invite each of you to start a beginner in this way, being careful to linger in the early stages of acquisition and to monitor any tensions or sub-optimal movements and correct them on a weekly basis. Such a beginning may take longer, but ease and balance are the rewards.

Early skills can be used in early compositions – created by the students themselves. For example, a young student of mine composed "Mrs. Piggy," her first piece, using third finger:

Activities like these not only help the student develop the necessary skills, but are highly motivational.

Third, return to the octave frame after extensions up or down:

I remember reading Raphael Bronstein's book, *The Science of Violin Playing*, in which he states that when the first finger is in the low position, it creates a situation in which subsequent playing of the third finger will either be slightly below the pitch, or will stretch the hand out of the basic frame. [Bronstein, 1981, p 6]

After experimenting for many years, I have begun teaching students to release the base of the first finger after playing low first finger, by letting the hand "spring" back to the octave frame. I have found that if I touch the student's bow on top of the stick, thereby immobilizing the bow, after the low first finger has played, it gives the hand time to organize itself and come back into the frame before going on to the next note. Of course, this begins building a motor program that insists that the hand is not under the stress of having the base of the first finger locked in the low position, while subsequently having to stretch to reach third and fourth fingers.

Notice how the third finger must extend itself when first finger is "locked" in the low position.

 This is the same principle that was applied to teaching the left elbow movement which slightly preceded the bow to each new string. By stopping the bow in much the same way, the left hand has time to return to its octave frame after extending back for a low first finger position. Eventually, the hand will adopt a fluid, coordinated movement. (See pp. 33-40 for discussion of this principle as it applies to left elbow movement.)

This photo shows the first finger in the low (extended back) position.

This photo shows the hand after "springing back" to the octave frame.

The hand comes back to the octave frame by releasing the base of the first finger.

The first time a student plays a low first finger in the Suzuki Violin School is "The Two Grenadiers" (Suzuki Violin School, Book 2). The hand should be well prepared before the student begins this piece by practicing Twinkle (or any other piece the teacher chooses) in the key of B-flat.

Twinkle in B-flat: At the *, stop the bow, release the inside edge of the hand and let it spring back to the octave frame.

Even though the student will play B-flat again, this movement keeps the hand from developing static tension, keeps the base of the hand light and easy against the neck, and prevents the hyperextension of the third and fourth fingers.

The Two Grenadiers: Check that the hand springs back to the basic octave frame after low first fingers.

The Two Grenadiers is a great teaching piece for this technique because low ones are consistently followed by an open string in the first several measures. These open strings present a perfect opportunity for the hand to spring back to the octave frame.

Fourth, use harmonics to teach shifting:

We all know that the hand should unweight during shifts, but getting the student's hand to actually do it is somewhat difficult. I remember my teacher and mentor, John Kendall, who said that it is the job of teachers to try to "create a no-fail environment." It occurred to me that if students had to hear a harmonic during their shifts, it might help teach the body what it needs to learn. The other benefit from this is that the bow must maintain in good contact with the string in order to produce the harmonic.

After my students can sing major and minor scales and play them in one and two octaves, I begin teaching them to play one octave scales on one finger on one string, with a harmonic slide between each note.

This is an example of a one octave scale on one finger and one string. Although the rhythm is indicated in dotted quarters and eighths, it is only a **RELATIVE** relationship. The important teaching point here is not the rhythm, but the harmonic, which must clearly be heard at each shift, or *. The scale progresses to all strings (E, D and G) and then to all fingers (first, third and fourth).

Both teacher and student make sure the fingers stay soft, separated and curved, with fourth finger curved over the string. The thumb travels with the hand on each shift throughout the scale. I teach going up initially (because movement toward the body is easier and more accurate than movement away from the body) and add coming down the scale **ONLY** when the student can go up in easy, light, accurate movements. A more complete description of this can be found in the Journal of the Suzuki Association of the Americas: *"Teaching Scales to the Young Student - One Approach"* by Susan Kempter. [American Suzuki Journal, August, 1992, Vol 20, No 4]

After the student can easily play one octave scales on all four fingers and on all four strings in this manner, I introduce standard 3-octave scales, still insisting on harmonic shifts for a long time. When it is apparent that the body of the student has adopted the harmonic, then it can be sped up so the harmonic is inaudible. This approach has greatly improved the ability of my students to shift accurately and lightly.

Fifth, teaching vibrato:

When the left hand is in the octave frame, the thumb should rest lightly against the neck of the violin. This posture restricts movement of the joint at the base of the thumb to one axis: back and forth. If the thumb exerts too much pressure against the neck, three undesirable side effects may result: 1. The back and forth movement is restricted, 2. The tip of the thumb may absorb the pressure by pushing against the neck, which forces the thumb to bend outward, away from the violin. This position can result in unrelenting static tension in the thumb, which in turn restricts ease of movement and can cause injury, or 3. The end of the thumb can push itself onto the neck of the violin, causing a deep bend of the last joint and tremendous tension in the thumb.

Really, the first vibrato lessons are those in which the student learns left elbow movement and shifting preparations like slides and harmonic slides. When getting down to the nitty-gritty of teaching vibrato, however, instead of shaking bottles and forcing the hand against the shoulder of the violin (which imposes a "hand" vibrato), I begin teaching awareness of how joints move.

The student must learn what a tension-free back and forth movement feels like. This can be accomplished in several ways, some of which will already be familiar:

1. With the left hand in the octave frame, have the student lift the left fingers slightly over the A string. Keeping the thumb gently against the neck of the violin, move the fingers OVER

the A string as far as they will go up and down the length of the string. Explore the student's active range of motion being sure that there is no tension in the base of the thumb, the wrist or the fingers. Make sure all fingers, including the fourth finger, stay soft, separate from each other and curved **OVER** the string.

2. In the octave frame, put a tissue under the second, or second and third fingers. Again, keep all fingers soft, separate and curved. Repeat the above motion with the hand gliding lightly on the piece of tissue. Check that the joint at the base of the thumb is soft and moving freely.

3. "Polishing the string." Do exactly the same motion as #2 above, but without the tissue.

The above three exercises produce a movement pattern like that in the following two photographs.

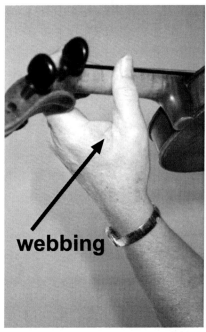

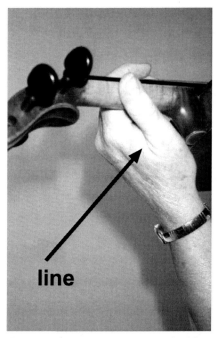

Backward movement of the hand exposes the stretched skin between the thumb and hand. I call this "webbing."

Forward movement of the hand produces a line.

I like this approach because it teaches the base joint of the thumb to be flexible. Also, as each student experiments, the natural tendency to vibrate USING THE ARM, OR THE HAND will emerge, allowing the development of the motion which is initially more natural for the student..

Each of the above steps may take several weeks or months, depending on the student. The crucial point is to linger in each until the child's hand has acquired ease, consistency and predictability before going to the next step. Each step might also be done with the violin in a "guitar hold," so students can monitor and refine their own movements.

After the thumb joint is trained, I begin teaching the joints of the fingers. This movement comes from adding a tiny amount of weight on the finger being trained and watching the hinges of the finger move freely. This step takes the longest, as the body tries to figure out exact balances between small muscles, tendons and joints. The important thing is to keep the movement under conscious control for as long as it takes. Conscious control is a hallmark of closed-loop movement. Lingering here allows the student to benefit from months and months of refinement. An easy way to help the student in a closed-loop situation is to make continual suggestions: "Let's try a fatter vibrato today." "How about a slower vibrato on fourth finger?" "Try to get the same movement on all four fingers this week." All these are ways to keep the student's vibrato under conscious control. The longer we linger in this stage, the more secure and the more varied vibratos the student will eventually produce.

Even though teaching the "vibrato hinge" (the hinge closest to the fingernail) takes a long time for some students, if they understand what to look and feel for, they will eventually get comfortable. Just like teaching the thumb hinge, rushing through any stage may cause frustration later on.

After acquisition of the student's natural vibrato, the "other" vibratos will also be introduced so students can vibrate with either the traditional hand or arm vibratos using a variety of widths and speeds.

Begin developing awareness of the "vibrato hinge" as soon as you begin teaching the joint at the base of the thumb. Devise ways to isolate this hinge and find its active range of motion. Three approaches that I have successfully used are:

1. Place the tip of the thumb just behind the "vibrato hinge" (the joint closest to the fingernail), leaving the tip of the finger free to move. Place the tip of the finger into the palm of the right hand. Move the right hand up and down.

2. Have student sit at a table. Place all 4 fingertips on the table (all fingers will be deeply curved and separate). Pretend the tips of the fingers are little suction cubs and that the fingers have no bones. Move the hand forward (making the finger joints bend deeply) and backward (letting them straighten slightly). There should be no excess weight on the fingertips, so easy, flexible movements are felt in the fingers

3. Watch the angles of the fingernail while the student vibrates without the bow. The backward motion of the hand causes the fingernail to be almost flat, or horizontal. The forward motion of the hand causes the fingernail to be almost perpendicular to the string.

Letting the vibrato go under automatic control too early may produce the body's answer to a fast, repetitive motion – a tremor – which is commonly called a "nanny goat" vibrato. If this gets adopted, undoing it and teaching a usable variety of vibratos can be exasperating for student and teacher, and is another example of proactive interference.

Be sure to watch the left wrist when the fourth finger is vibrating. It should be in a soft posture that allows the fourth to come to the string in a soft curve. The tendency for the wrist to extend itself out is a reaction to the weaker finger and can cause the finger to come down with too much force, or create tension in the wrist itself. Photos of this can be seen on page 43.

Teach the complete vibrato cycle WITHOUT the bow. Adding the bow too early overloads working memory and usually produces tensions in the left hand because the student will try for more speed than the hand has been trained for. When the hand has acquired ease with BOTH movements (the base of the thumb and the vibrato hinge), add the bow in the following manner:

1. Place the bow on the string AT THE TIP, but do not move it.

2. Have the student give full attention to the newly developed vibrato movement, and when it is fluid, balanced and easy,

3. Move the bow all the way to the frog with the bow arm moving exactly as it has been trained.

4. Stop. Shake out both hands and arms and repeat with up-bows only. Remember: up-bows bring the bow arm and hand closer to the body (adduction), which is an easier and more accurate movement.

5. Add down-bows only when the body has acquired the up-bow movement patterns.

This teaching approach may appear on the surface as slow and pedantic, but remember that the vibrato segment of each student's lesson might only take one or two minutes. The rest of the lesson can be devoted to music-making at the student's highest level.

Also, the reward of a vibrato which has been kept under conscious control (closed-loop movement) for as long as possible is that students develop the ability to play with a variety of vibrato widths and speeds – depending on what the music and their personal tastes require. Isn't that more satisfying in the end?

Things to think about . . .

1. Our brains make sense of the world by organizing things into patterns. These can be patterns of speech, movement, behaviour or thinking. Proactive interference is one way that these patterns can be disrupted.

   Most violin teachers are familiar with the following Minuet from Anna Magdalena's notebook by J.S. Bach.

Example #1. Play this as written:

That was easy.

Now, challenge yourself to not only play it in duple rhythm, but try to feel and hear it in duple rhythm, as in Example #2 on the next page:

Example #2:

This presents more of a challenge. The moment we stop absolute concentration, we revert to triple meter with the attendant emphasis on the macro beats.

2. Recall your own development as a violinist. Did you ever have need to re-do a skill or technique that your muscles had already acquired? As nearly as possible (including what it was that needed changing, your strategies to change it, frustrations you encountered, and a rough time line until your body got retrained), refer to Fitt's Stages (p. 78) and give a detailed analysis of your re-training experience as it relates to each of his three stages.

Conclusion

It is hoped that this book will foster ideas, and generate experimentation and communication among violin teachers – all of which have the potential to improve the profession for all of us.

— Susan Kempter

Sources

Bronstein, Raphael. 1981. The Science of Violin Playing. Paganiniana Publications, Inc. Neptune City, New Jersey.

Dickinson, J. 1985. *Some Perspectives on Motor Learning Theory.* in Differing Perspectives in Motor Learning, Memory and Control. D. Goodman, R.B. Wilberg & I.M. Franks, eds. Elsevier Science Publishers B.V., Amsterdam, The Netherlands.

Floyd, R.T. and Thompson, Clem. 1998. Manual of Structural Kinesiology. WCB/McGraw-Hill,USA.

Hannaford, Carla. 1995. Smart Moves: Why Learning is not All in Your Head. Great Ocean Publishers. Arlington, Virginia.

Lane, Norman E. 1987. Skill Acquisition Rates and Patterns: Issues and Training Implications Springer-Verlag. New York.

Lee & Magill. 1985. *Can Forgetting Facilitate Skill Acquisition?* in Differing Perspectives In Motor Learning, Memory and Control. D. Goodman; R. Wilberg & I. M. Franks, eds. Elsevier Science Publications B.V., Amsterdam, The Netherlands.

Medoff, Lynn, M.A., M.P.T. *The Importance of Movement Education in the Training of Young Violinists.* Medical Problems of Performing Artists. December, 1999.

Miller, G.A. *The Magical Number Seven, Plus or Minus Two: Some Limits on Our Capacity for Processing Information.* Psychological Review. 63; 1956. 81-97.

Rolland, Paul and Mutschler, Marla. 1974. The Teaching of Action in String Playing. Boosey & Hawkes, Inc., USA.

Sosniak, Lauren. 1990. *From Tyro to Virtuoso.* in Music and Child Development: Biology of Music Making - Proceedings of the 1987 Denver Conference. Frank R. Wilson & Franz L. Roehmann, eds. MMB Music, Inc., St. Louis, Missouri. 274-290.

Southern California Orthopedic Institute. *Rotator Cuff Disease/Impingement.* Retrieved 9/6/01 from http://www.scoi.com/cuffdise.html#1.

Stein, Charles Jay. 2000. *The Alexander Technique for Musicians.* Retrieved 8/30/01 from http://alexandertechnique.com/articles/stein

Wolkomir, Richard. *When the Work You Do Ends Up Costing You an Arm and a Leg.* Smithsonian. Vol 25, No. 3; June. 1994. 90-103.

Wilson, Frank R. 1986. Tone Deaf and All Thumbs? An Invitation to Music-Making. Vintage Books [a division of Random House], New York, New York.

Wilson, Frank R., & Roehmann, Franz. 1992. *The Study of Biomechanical and Physiological Processes in Relation to Musical Performance.* in The Handbook of Research on Music Teaching and Learning. 509-534. Richard Colwell, ed. MENC/Schirmer Books, New York.

Wulf, G. & Schmidt, R. 1994. *Feedback-Induced Variability and the Learning of Generalized Motor Programs.* Journal of Motor Behavior. Vol 26, no 4, 348-361.

Notes